PICK UP AND RUN ASSEMBLIES 1

Fifteen easy assemblies for primary schools:
minimum preparation, maximum effect!

Nick Harding

kevin
mayhew

First published in 2004 by

KEVIN MAYHEW LTD
Buxhall, Stowmarket, Suffolk, IP14 3BW
E-mail: info@kevinmayhewltd.com

Some of these assemblies were first published by First and Best in Education Ltd, Earlstrees Court, Earlstrees Road, Corby, Northants NN17 4AX.

9 8 7 6 5 4 3

ISBN 978 1 84417 296 2
Catalogue No. 1500724

Edited and typeset by Graham Harris
Cover design by Angela Selfe

Printed and bound in Great Britain

Contents

Each assembly has an object to focus on	Using the object, you can then explore the theme

Introduction

There are times in every teacher's working life when time and inspiration are both lacking. There may be a pile of jobs to do, parents to see and displays to mount, and the added distraction of preparing an assembly. This book aims to solve one of those problems, with plenty of pick-up-and-run ideas for any teacher to use.

Using props to focus the children's attention, each assembly has clear messages which are easily understood. Here, among other items, you will find a bandage, a pair of men's shoes, bread, a police hat and the world. All these will help put a clear and memorable message across to your children.

Object: Person
Theme: Humanity 1

Theme Everybody is special and individual.

You will need A volunteer to stand at the front all the way through.

Introduction Here is a person. He/she is different to everyone else.
This person has a unique appearance, unique thought patterns, unique personality and unique attitudes. Like all of you, there is no one quite like him/her.

Active game *Find the person*
Ask the children to look towards or point at anyone they see who fulfils the description you give. Find the person with:

- a bright shirt
- a big smile
- long hair
- the oldest-looking face
- the coolest clothes
- a dark pair of trousers
- a watch
- stripes on their clothes

Game *My friend*
Ask two children who are friends to volunteer. One leaves the room while you ask the other this list of questions about

him/her. Then the child returns and tries to answer the questions with the same answers. Then the children swop over and the game is repeated.

What does he/she like to eat?

What is his/her favourite TV programme?

What does he/she really dislike at school?

Does he/she have any brothers or sisters?

Where would he/she love to go on holiday?

Talk

Who has brothers or sisters? Are they exactly the same as you? It's really exciting that we are all different and unique.

When we were all finding the person, none of us found someone who was completely identical to us. Even the two friends who just played *My friend* are not the same.

Christians believe that all people are made by God, and we are all different. Yet God himself came to live as a person and find out what it is like for us.

Illustration

Ask the children to imagine they are at a Christmas party, whatever time of year it is! Have a few balloons, some nibbles and a few small presents. Give these out to some of the children, and encourage them all to think a little more about Christmas parties.

Then ask the children what they think Christmas is all about. Point out that the whole reason for Christmas is to celebrate the birth of God's Son coming down to earth as a human.

Story

Read this account of what happened to the baby Jesus, which is taken from the Bible. You may want to start by mentioning that it was traditional at that time for babies to be presented to the priests in the temple a few weeks after birth, but that custom is not common now.

‘Simeon was a wise old man. Some people thought he was a prophet, and a messenger from God. He lived and worked in the temple, but was almost too old to do much. But always in the back of his mind was the message he thought God had given him years before, that one day he would see the new King, the Son of God.

He was sure that God had spoken to him and told him to expect a special baby, who would save the world. Little did he know what was about to happen.

Meanwhile, Jesus had been born, and after a few weeks his parents, Mary and Joseph, decided it was time to take him to the temple to be presented. They got everything ready and set off to walk there.

When Mary and Joseph arrived at the temple they saw an old man rushing towards them. Simeon was really excited, and as soon as he saw Jesus he knew that this was the baby God had told him to look out for. After asking Mary and Joseph, he took the baby Jesus in his arms.

Simeon was sure that the time had come at last, and he had seen the new King that God had promised so long before. He thanked God that finally the waiting was over and the world would be saved.

Mary and Joseph watched and listened. Even though they knew their baby was special they didn’t fully understand what was being said. Simeon, meanwhile, now knew that he could rest and relax. He had seen God’s promised Son at last.’

Closing

We all know that Jesus was special, but so was Simeon and so are we. Everyone is special, and that's the nature of humanity. Ask the children why they think God sent his Son Jesus to be born as a baby in a dirty, smelly stable. Why did Jesus have to live as a normal baby and child? We can never say that no one, not even God, understands the things we feel or suffer. Christians believe that God understands because, through his Son Jesus, he went through it all too.

Prayer

Ask the children to listen to this prayer and pray themselves in their minds:

Thank you that we are all different.
Thank you that you know how we feel.
Thank you that you lived as a child and an adult.
Thank you that you know how we feel.
Amen.

Object: Letter
Theme: Worry

2

Theme

Worry isn't good for us.

You will need

A letter, a sheet of paper or white board and marker pen, the letters which spell out the words *worry, lost, sad,* and *help* on separate pieces of paper.

Introduction

Have a letter in your pocket or on a nearby table and as the children arrive pretend to read it, with lots of comments like: 'Oh dear' and 'That's not very good'. Then look up and explain to the children that you are reading a letter from your Aunty Freda, who is having a hard time. She has been ill, her cat has left home, the boiler for the central heating has stopped working, and she fell through her favourite chair! Explain that there's not much you can do to help because Aunty Freda lives a long way away, but you do worry about her. In fact, you worry about lots of things . . . like what to say in assembly!

Active game

Losing and finding

Put up these letters on the wall of the room with Blu-Tack –
W, O, R, R, Y, L, O, S, T, S, A, D, H, E, L, P
Ask for a child near each one to take it off the wall and bring it to the front. Then arrange the children so the words are clear to those watching (and then stick the words up at the front).

WORRY, LOST, SAD, HELP

Game *The brick game*

Using a foam brick, inflatable mallet or something similar, play this simple word association game. A pair of children compete to win. The child who hesitates for too long or repeats a word that has already been used is called '*out*' and tapped on the head or back (very gently, and check with the headteacher first!). Play rounds on the following subjects:

- Losing something special
- Being scared
- Things I worry about
- Being upset

Discussion Talk about a time when you lost something of value or importance, and tell the children how you felt about it. You may want to invite them to talk about losing things and how it makes them feel. How did they, or would they, go about finding the object that was lost?

Story Read out this story.

> 'Charlie the sheep was part of a big family. They spent most of their time happily playing and eating in the fields. One day Charlie was bored and wanted to do some exploring, so he wandered away from the others. He walked a long way across fields, bridges and lanes, through valleys, woods and streams. He was very far from the others when he began to feel hungry, and before long the sky started to get dark. It was then that Charlie realised he had no idea where he had come from or which way he should go to get back to his family. To put it

bluntly, he was lost. As he thought about what to do and ran this way and that he became increasingly worried and frightened, and finally slumped down and cried.

After lying still and weeping for a while it was so dark that Charlie could hardly see anything, and the breeze was rustling in the trees. Then he heard a noise. As he crouched down his heart pounded. Was it a wolf? Could it be a lion? Would he survive? He was really worried now, and so scared that he couldn't even move. Charlie plucked up all his courage and opened his eyes, looking towards the noise. But he didn't see a wolf or a lion. Instead he saw the familiar face of the shepherd coming to take him home.

Later Charlie sat cosy and warm in the arms of the shepherd, listening to the bleating of all his friends. ’

Quiz

Read out the story a second time, this time slipping in some wrong words. Ask the children to go '*baaa*' if they spot a word that was not in the original story.

For example: 'Charlie the dog was part of a big family. They spent most of their money happily playing . . . '

Discussion

Talk about how Charlie felt at different stages of the story. He moved from feeling bored to being brave and adventurous, and then to being scared, worried and lonely. Then ask about the things that worry or concern the children. Ask what they do when they feel like this. Who do they turn to, and how do they get help?

In the story the shepherd went out of his way to help Charlie.

There are always people around to help us when we get worried. Teachers will help us, and so will other staff at school, those who look after us at home, and many other people. So if you're worried about anything, it's best to get help.

This is a similar story to one Jesus told, and he called himself the Good Shepherd. Jesus wanted people to know that he is willing to be a shepherd for us, finding us and helping us when we struggle. Because he loves us he will go out of his way to help us.

Prayer Remind the children of the words on the wall (*worry, lost, sad,* and *help*). On a sheet of paper or board make a list of some of the things that worry or concern the children in the class/school. Then pray this prayer, repeating it and filling in the gaps with the children's concerns:

Thank you, Jesus, that you called yourself the Good Shepherd. You look after us all, even when we feel ___________ . Help us to ask you for help when we are worried about things.

Amen.

Object: Torch
Theme: Journey of life

3

Theme We need help to find our way on the journey through life.

You will need A torch.

Introduction Ask the children what they might want to use a torch for. For example, you could use a torch for looking in a dark cupboard for something, or to help you find your way in the dark. Torches give light to dark places, and help us find the right way.

Illustration Ask all the children to lower their heads, close their eyes and cover their faces with their hands. Then ask them to count to eight out loud while you move quietly to another part of the room. Then, with their eyes still closed, ask them to point to where they think you are now standing. It's not easy to see in the dark! When you're in the dark a torch helps.

Game *Balancing act*

Get two volunteers out, and ask them to get into the following positions. The one who does it best and balances longest is the winner:

- stand on one leg
- stand on two legs and a hand
- stand on one leg and one hand
- balance on your back

- balance on your bottom and one foot
- stand on both knees and hands but no feet

Discussion

Ask the children to think about and discuss the following things and how they help us find the right way to go and the right things to do:

- Torch
- Police
- Map
- Parent/carer

Story

Before you tell the story ask the children to listen out carefully for the different ways the characters find the right direction to go.

> ‘They knew it wasn’t going to be an easy journey, but they had no idea how hard it would get! Charlotte and ~~Adam~~ Simon were on their way to a cottage for a holiday, with their mum and dad. Mum was driving, and the traffic had been awful. Dad sat mumbling about the awful roads and reading the instructions telling him how to find the cottage, while the children argued and moaned on the back seat.
>
> They had been stuck on the same stretch of motorway for ages, and Charlotte kept asking: ‘Are we nearly there yet?’ which didn’t help! Finally they were moving, and after another hour in which it had turned from sunny to dark evening, Dad said: ‘It must be time to turn off the motorway soon. I’ll look at the map.’ He turned on the light in the car to see, and sure

enough the next junction was the one for them. As they turned right, following signs for the nearest town, they felt a little more relaxed.

Mum said: 'Nearly there. We'll soon be in the cottage in the warm – there'll be a fire lit ready for us', in the hope that ~~Adam~~ Simon and Charlotte would stop arguing!

But as they passed through the town the road got narrower, there were lanes off left and right, and Dad was confused. 'Ring Aunty Joan on the mobile,' suggested Mum. 'She knows how to find the cottage.'

'Turn right past the farm with the big barn,' Aunty Joan instructed, and that's what they did, but then the car started to slow down and Mum said: 'There's no power – the car's stopping!'

Dad told her to stop and then, looking at the panel next to the clock, Mum realised what the problem was – there was no petrol left! Dad was really cross, but ~~Adam~~ Simon and Charlotte were really pleased.

They grabbed their torches, put on their coats, and got ready to find the cottage by torchlight. But they didn't really know which way to go until ~~Adam~~ Simon said: 'I can smell smoke,' and headed off along the lane into some woods. And there, at the end of the torch beam, was a little cottage with smoke coming from the chimney and a light on inside.

'Well, we've found something,' said Dad, catching up with ~~Adam~~ Simon. 'Let's hope it's the right cottage!'

Quiz

Split the children into two teams, and ask the following questions:

1. What was the first item they used to find the way to the cottage?
   (*Instructions*)
2. Who gives us directions at school?
   (*Teachers, etc.*)
3. Who gives us directions at home?
   (*Carer, parents, etc.*)
4. Name another item in the car which helped them.
   (*Light, map, mobile phone*)
5. What happened to stop the car?
   (*No fuel*)
6. What two things helped ~~Adam~~ Simon find the cottage?
   (*Smoke smell, torch*)

Closing

To find the right way to do things and the way to live our lives we need help, not only from torches and maps! We need the help of each other and those who care about us. It's best not to try to do it all ourselves but to ask if we need help.

Prayer idea

Ask the children to sit quietly and remember times when others have helped them do something or find their way somewhere.

Object: A cross
Theme: **Failure**

4

Theme We all go wrong and let ourselves down.

You will need A large cross, such as those put on the pages of wrong or unsatisfactory work!

Introduction Have any of you ever got this on your work? (*Hold up a cross*) I used to when I was your age! It's a terrible feeling to know that you have failed to do something, yet none of us can do everything perfectly – not even teachers! We all fail and go wrong by doing or saying things we know we shouldn't. If we do go wrong there is a chance that we can put it right by trying again, saying sorry, and being forgiven.

Active game *Simon says . . .*

This age-old game remains popular with children of all backgrounds. Ask the children to stand (if there is space) and do whatever you preface with '*Simon says*'. If you do not preface it with these words they should not do it. You may want to play competitively and have some children sitting out, or you may want to play it totally for fun. Some of the things that can be done in limited space include:

standing	*hands on head*
sitting	*standing on one leg*

touching elbow, etc. *hopping*
jumping *shaking*

Discussion The game was all about following instructions, and you could have been out if you had got it wrong. We all go wrong, and do things which we should regret. Often we know that we've done something wrong because we feel guilty.

Ask the children what things they do that are wrong. Try to help them focus on things that are real to them (fighting at school) rather than bigger things that they know to be wrong (murder, etc.). Ask them how it feels if someone does something that is against them or hurts them.

Game *Yes/no challenge*

Individual children (perhaps three or four) should come to the front and must answer questions for 30 seconds without saying 'yes' or 'no'. If they do they have gone wrong and are out of the game. This is great fun, and bears repeating later in the assembly if there is time.

Story *Zacchaeus*

This story is best told with all the group involved in the presentation of the story and given a role to play. One person can come out to the front to play Jesus, another play Zacchaeus, and the others stay sitting where they are to become the crowd. The crowd should respond to the other characters' names as follows:

Zacchaeus 'What a nasty man!'

Jesus 'What a great man!'

At the end of the story the response to Zacchaeus' name needs to change to 'What a changed man!' to reinforce the change in his life.

Use these main points of the story, and fill it in to suit the children in your situation:

> ‘The whole town was excited because they had heard that the famous man, Jesus, was coming their way. They had heard that Jesus could heal people of diseases and illnesses, and that he was very wise and clever.
>
> Zacchaeus was a small, unpopular man, and everyone hated him.
>
> Zacchaeus was a tax collector who kept money for himself and acted in a selfish and dishonest way.
>
> Jesus was visiting his village with a large crowd, all calling out and surrounding Jesus and the travellers with him.
>
> Zacchaeus was at the back of the crowd and couldn't get a view of Jesus, so he climbed a tree to see what was going on.
>
> Despite the crowd, Jesus saw Zacchaeus and asked him to come down and talk. Zacchaeus invited Jesus to go to his house for tea.
>
> Jesus knew all about how Zacchaeus had been stealing money off the people in the town, and told Zacchaeus he could only put things right and be forgiven if he gave the money back.
>
> Zacchaeus knew that he had done wrong and promised to change, which he did. He returned all the money and some more to the people he had tricked.’

Discussion Ask the children why they think Jesus forgave Zacchaeus. What evidence was there that Zacchaeus had changed? Link the discussion of Zacchaeus with our own situations. We all go wrong and do things which we should not. If we are truly sorry, we can be forgiven by others, which gives us the chance to make a new start. (*Lift up the cross*) A new start gives us a chance to replace this cross with a tick!

Prayer Ask the children to sit quietly for two minutes, looking at the cross shape and thinking of the things in their own lives that need forgiveness. Remind them that we can all change and start again.

Object: Posters
Theme: Other people

5

Theme No one is worthless, we all have value.

You will need Posters of some famous people (pop stars, sports stars, etc.).

Game *What do I do?*

Ask some extrovert children to come to the front. Children take it in turn to act out or mime the following jobs and pastimes in front of the rest of the group. The other children try to guess what they are. It may help you to have cards with the answers written on them to hold up when they have guessed correctly.

Pop star	*Motorbike rider*
Footballer	*Woodworker/Carpenter*
Fisherman	*Cricketer*
Sewing	*Mountain climber*
Swimmer	*Teacher*

Discussion Which of those activities do the children enjoy doing? Which of them would they like to spend a day doing? Which person would they like to be their best friend?

There are some people who we like to go around with and others that we do not. Friendships are often based on what we enjoy doing together as well as personalities. For instance, the Queen is not likely to go out to tea with your teacher. She will have her own friends to spend time with.

(*Hold up some of the posters*) We might think we know some of these people, but really we don't, and they don't know us. They have their own friends, and they make mistakes and do good things just like the rest of us. They might have more money, but that does not make them better people.

The Bible tells us about Jesus, who was the Son of God. Yet Jesus mixed with all sorts of people, those who thought they were good and those who knew they were bad!

Quiz

Anagrams

Read out the letters for each of these types of people slowly word by word, and ask the children to remember each letter from each word and work out what the word is before you go on to the next one.

RCIH (*rich*)	CKIS (*sick*)
CEVERL (*clever*)	DLO (*old*)
ROPO (*poor*)	GOUNY (*young*)
DETHA (*hated*)	DAS (*sad*)
DLIBN (*blind*)	MEAL (*lame*)

Jesus did not just go around with one type of person. He wanted to talk and help everyone. So Jesus went around with all those types of people and more.

Story

The healing of the ten lepers

Before you read the story explain the attitude that prevailed to those with skin diseases like leprosy. Mention that they had to shout to warn people to move out of their way, and how hurt they must have felt to be shunned by their communities.

> ‘Jesus was travelling again; he was always travelling! This time he was on his way to the important city of Jerusalem, and as usual a large

crowd of people were going with him, eager to see what he did and hear what he had to say. As he walked along the crowd stopped and started to mutter. There were some lepers – ten of them with the dreaded skin disease – coming towards them. 'Go away, you're not welcome!' shouted some of the crowd, while others turned around and walked away from them. 'We're not going near them,' they said. 'We don't want our skin and limbs to go rotten!'

Jesus stopped and waited for the ten lepers to come near him. 'Heal us, master!' they said. 'We know you can!' Jesus spoke to them about how much they trusted him, and then he said: 'Go away and tell your friends and leaders. If you trust me you will be made well and your skin will heal.' The men turned and started to walk home, slowly and a little confused. But after a while their skin started to change colour and heal, and before long they were all as normal and well as anyone else!

Meanwhile Jesus and the others continued on their walk to Jerusalem, the crowd puzzled about what had happened to the lepers. Then one of them came running back and threw himself at his feet. 'You have made us all well!' said the leper. 'Thank you so much!' Jesus looked at him. 'It's a shame that there's only one of you who has come back to thank me. Where are the others?' he said. The man left to go home and tell his family the amazing news while Jesus continued on his journey. ,

Quiz

Split the children into two groups. Ask the following questions one by one, giving time for the group to decide on the answer quietly. Then ask one of the groups, and if they get it wrong ask the other:

- Where was Jesus going to? (*Jerusalem*)
- How many lepers were there? (*Ten*)
- What did leprosy do to the skin? (*Made it go rotten*)
- What happened when lepers approached others? (*They moved away*)
- Who did Jesus tell them to go to see? (*Friends and leaders*)
- How many went back to see Jesus? (*One*)
- What did the man say to Jesus? (*Thank you*)
- What did Jesus say? (*Why is there only one? Where are the others?*)

Talk and discussion

Ask the children how they would have felt if they had really been the lepers mentioned in the story. (*Hold up posters*) It must be good to be famous like these people, but really awful to be hated like the lepers in the story.

Jesus helped the lepers, even though most people hated and feared them. Jesus showed his love to all people, whatever their background and whatever they were suffering. It seems sad that only one leper bothered to return to say 'thank you' to Jesus.

Jesus gives us an example of how we should treat the people around us. We should go out of our way to care for them even if other people can't be bothered.

Invite the children to make suggestions of situations where they could help people who are modern 'outcasts'.

Prayer

Ask all the children to think about names at the appropriate times:

My name is _______ . Thank you, Jesus, that you care for me.

My brothers and sisters are _______ . Thank you, Jesus, that you care for them. Help me to care for them too.

My friends are _______ . Thank you, Jesus, that you care for them. Help me to care for them too.

Thank you, Jesus, that you care for the people around us, whether they are famous or unloved. Help me to care for them too.

Amen.

Talk and discussion

It may be worth contacting a mission or aid agency such as The Leprosy Mission to find out about the problems caused by leprosy today <www.leprosymission.org.uk>

✓ 18·9·09

Object: Bandage
Theme: Pain
6

Theme We all get hurt by others, and we should all learn to forgive.

You will need A bandage.

Introduction What do we use a bandage for? We might hurt ourselves and bandage ourselves up, or get treatment from someone else. We can use the bandage even if someone else hurts us. But what can we do if someone hurts us inside by the things they do or say? We can't bandage our heart or our feelings until they get better!

Game *'And' and 'but'*

Ask for a volunteer. The child must talk to you and answer your questions for one minute without saying *'and'* or *'but'*. If they do they are out of the game straight away and another child has a go. Repeat this with other volunteers, depending on time.

Talk In the game we just played if someone made a mistake they were automatically out of the game, and there was no way back in. There was no chance of 'forgiveness'.

Story and activity Read this story, stopping at the appropriate points and asking: 'What would you have done?', allowing some of the children to make suggestions.

'Steve and Ben were both in the same class at school. They lived in the same town and in the same street. They walked along the same road to school at the same time each day. They supported the same football team, liked the same music, and watched the same TV programmes. They were very good friends, and played together each evening after school.

One day Ben was excited. It was nearly his birthday and he really really wanted a new bike. On the day itself his mum bought him a shiny new bike and said he could go out on it after school.

When school ended Steve and Ben dashed out as fast as they could. They ran across the playground, through the gates, tore down the road, and turned onto their street puffing and panting. In no time Ben and Steve had got changed and were ready to go off cycling, Steve on his old battered bike and Ben on his shiny new one.

They raced around the park, but Ben won time and time again because Steve's chain kept coming off. Steve asked for a go on the new bike, but Ben refused.

What would you have done?

Then Ben had to go home to have a birthday tea with his family, and Steve was left sitting on his bike wondering what to do.

As he sat there a bad idea crept into his head. 'Why don't I just borrow Ben's bike for a few minutes?' he thought, looking at the sparkling new bike leaning on the wall. 'No one will know.'

What would you have done?

Steve got off his bike and quietly sneaked up to Ben's house, wheeling the bike away and jumping on as he pushed it into the road. It was as smooth, as fast and as great to ride as he had imagined. He rode down the road and, turning the corner, lost control on some oil. The bike swung from under him and shot over the road into the path of a car. The driver slammed on his brakes but it was too late as the front wheel was squashed.

What would you have done?

As Steve got up and dusted himself down he looked over and was horrified. He was nearly in tears as he took the bike back to Ben's house and faced his angry mum, and saw how much he had upset his friend. But Ben was really good about it.

What would you have done?

'I know it was an accident,' he said. 'I'll soon get it mended and then I'll be able to ride it again.' Steve went home feeling a little happier, and the next day they were as good friends as they had always been.

It was only a few days later when Ben and Steve were playing football with Steve's new ball, and Ben kicked it onto the railway line. There was no way they could get it back.

What would you have done?

Steve was furious with Ben, stormed off, and would not even speak to him the next day at school. Ben thought that was unfair, especially after Steve had ruined his new bike.

What would you have done? ’

Discussion

Discuss with the children how Steve and Ben acted in the story. Ask and answer the following questions:

- Was what Ben did in forgiving Steve right or wrong?
- Was Steve right to borrow the bike without asking?
- Should Steve have forgiven Ben after the ball was lost?

Closing

(*Hold up the bandage*) There are times for all of us when others hurt us. Some of you may be feeling hurt even now by what someone has said or done to you today. A bandage isn’t going to take the hurt away and it is no use holding on to that hurt, because it may never go away if you do. The best and kindest thing to do is to forgive, even though it’s not always easy.

Prayer idea

Ask the children to sit quietly and think about people who have hurt them. Ask them to think about how good it is to forgive others.

Object: Phone
Theme: Communication 7

Theme To keep any friendship or relationship going we need to be able to communicate effectively.

You will need A telephone.

Active game *Captain's aboard*

Assign different areas of the room to be the *port, starboard, forward* and *aft*. When these names are called out the children have to point to the appropriate area. Further actions and instructions can be added:

- *Captain's aboard* – stand and salute
- *Scrub the decks* – mime this action
- *Climb the rigging* – mime this action
- *Attend the lifeboats* – give someone a 'piggy back'

Introduction Have you ever thought what it would be like if the telephone hadn't been invented? We wouldn't be able to talk to our friends, our families, or people who can help us. Everything would take much longer because we would have to communicate by letter. Telephones help us keep in touch, and keeping in touch helps us to keep friendships and relationships going.

Discussion Bring out the point that when playing *Captain's aboard* we all needed to listen and act. Sometimes we have to listen extremely carefully to hear what messages are being given to us so that we can take the right action.

Ask the children to name as many different ways of sending and receiving messages as possible. They should include the following:

Telephone	*Fax*
Internet	*E-mail*
Talking	*Letter*
Newspaper	*Message through someone else*

Quiz Read out the following clues for different types of people that the children might talk to at some time. There are three clues per person. Award three points to the children and none to yourself if it is guessed after clue 1, two points to the children and one for yourself if it guessed after clue 2, and one point for the children and two for yourself if it is guessed after clue 3. Sadly you are unlikely to win!

1 They cook your food
2 They usually live with you
3 They write notes to school about you
(*Mum/Dad/Main carer*)

1 You see them most days, but not at weekends
2 They work in buildings full of children
3 Each class has one
(*Teacher*)

1 You probably have some here
2 They are not your relatives
3 You play with them
(*Friends*)

1 You give them money

2 A lot work in town centres

3 They sell things

(*Shopkeeper*)

Game *Chinese whispers*

Arrange at least six children in a line at the front of the class. Whisper a message to the first person and pass it along the line to the other end. Then see what the final message is and see how it differs from the original.

Story one

‘Sara and her mum lived together in a small flat. They got on well most of the time, but as Sara got older she hated her mum's nagging more and more! Her mum was always going on about keeping her room tidy, about what time she would be back, and about where she was going. One day it all got too much for Sara, and she shouted at her mum: ‘Why don't you just stop nagging me? Every time you speak to me you are nagging! Please, just don't talk to me.’ Sara's mum was very upset, but she decided to give it a try. Next day nothing was said over breakfast, and when her mum collected Sara from school they didn't say a word to each other. Sara felt bad. ‘Mum,’ she said later. ‘Please talk to me so that I know if you love me.’’

Story two

‘Jesus was getting ready to die! He knew that the time had come when he would be arrested and put to death on a cross made of rough wood. So he decided to talk to his Father, God. He went with his friends to a quiet hillside and asked them to pray, while he sat on his own and told

God how he felt. He was scared and didn't want to suffer, but he knew that he had to do it. He told God all the things on his mind. He knew it was good to communicate with the one he loved. '

Closing It is good to keep in contact with those we care about. Friends aren't really friends if we never talk or write to them. The phone is one good way of many to keep communicating with others, so that they can be helped by us and we can be helped by them. God is interested in hearing us talk to him, whatever we or others need. We should be able to talk to God about everything because he knows how we feel.

Prayer *Dear God,*
Thank you for all the people we can communicate with. Help us to keep communicating with our friends, our families, and those we care about.
Amen.

Object: Book
Theme: Special books 8

Theme Books are important, and some are special.

You will need A book that is special to you, and a sheet of paper or board for a game of '*Hangman*'.

Quiz *Hangman*
Divide the children into two teams, who take it in turns to guess the letters. They could score points for each correct word guessed, or only for guessing the whole book title.
Choose book titles that the majority of children should know, and ones taken from cartoon films. Here are some suggestions:

The Lion King	*James and the Giant Peach*
Harry Potter	*Finding Nemo*
The Bible	*Fantastic Mr Fox*
Babe	*The Worst Witch*

Talk (*Hold up and talk about the book you have*) This is my book. It's called _______ and I like it because _______ . It is special to me because _______ . Have any of you got any favourite books that are special to you? The Bible is a special book for many people, even those who don't really believe in God. It tells many stories and has poems, battles, advice and letters in it. Even Jesus thought the Bible was an important book to read and to learn.

Story one

'Many thousands of years ago there lived a king called David. He had grown up an ordinary boy in an ordinary family, and for some time he wrote songs and poems and played music for the old king called Saul. He always read parts of the Bible to help him and encourage him.

One day he was thinking about all the good things in the Bible and how it helped him do the right thing and learn the best way to live. He decided to put something about the words of God into the prayer he was writing, and so he thought about what the Bible was like. In the end he wrote: 'Your word is like a lamp to guide me and a light for the path so I can see the way.' This is now in the Bible and is part of a prayer called Psalm 119. The Bible was a special book for David.'

Discussion

Ask the children what different types of books they know and use. Consider what each type of book does and does not show. It may be useful to have a range of books available such as the ones here:

Road Atlas

Shows where you should be going, helps you plan a journey

Story book

To entertain and often to give a message

History book

Tells you what happened in the past

Song book

Gives us words and tunes to enjoy

Dictionary

Helps us find out more about things that interest us

Poetry book

Gives us words to enjoy and things to think about

Explain to the children that the Bible contains examples of all the books listed in some form. Whatever type of book we enjoy there is some of it in the Bible. But the Bible is like any other book – it is no good for us unless it is read by us!

Story two

'Zoe was asleep, lying with her eyes closed and her hands tight on her favourite story-book. She always looked at the same story-book before she went to bed, and she always had done since her grandad gave it to her. Zoe took the book away on holiday with her, and loved to read it after breakfast when there was time. The book had plenty of good stories and pictures in it. Now she could read the stories well, but when she was younger she had looked at the pictures while her grandad read them, word by word. Every time she looked at the book it reminded her of her grandad. It would always be a really special book to her.'

Conclusion

Books are really good, and for many of us some books are really special. The Bible is a special book for many people, but we all have special books for other reasons too. Don't just leave books on the shelf getting dusty – use them!

Thought idea

Ask the children to think about their favourite books in quiet, and to remember what those books mean to them.

Object: Membership card
Theme: **Clubs**

9

Theme It is important for all of us to belong.

You will need A membership card.

Introduction This is a membership card. Many of us are members of things that we don't need a membership card for. We are all members of our community – that's the area and the people around us. Every one of us here this morning/afternoon is a member of the school community. We might also be members of other clubs, teams and activities here in school and outside school. Who can guess what this membership card is for? It's for ________ . (explain your membership card as appropriate.)

Active game *Living statues*

Ask for a small group of volunteers to come out to the front. They must arrange themselves into a scene to depict one of the following things within a limited time. Then when you clap or blow a whistle they must freeze like statues. Some children may need to 'act' inanimate objects such as netball posts or bus seats.

A netball match	*A trip to the zoo*
A disco or party	*School at playtime*
A bus ride	*Sports day*

Discussion Ask the children about the game. Would it have worked if all the children had done their own thing and not worked as a team?

No one could have completed the scenes on their own. Then talk about the things it is fun to do with others, such as playing football and netball. It would be really boring to watch *Coronation Street, Eastenders* or another TV show if there was only one character in it (although we may think it's boring with many characters!)

Discussion activity Find out from the children what teams or groups they are in by naming some popular ones and asking children to stand if they are in them. They may include sports teams, clubs, cubs or brownies, etc. If we are part of a team we work together and help each other.

Game *My team*

Invite a child to come out to the front and talk for 30 seconds about a team or group they are in. If they stop before the time is up they are out of the game. Repeat this with as many of the children as possible and even teachers. It is surprisingly difficult!

Talk and story Jesus was part of a team, with his disciples helping him and being his friends. One thing they always did was go to the temple (church) together, and join the others who wanted to talk to God, sing to him and worship him. Jesus had been going to the temple to worship ever since he was a little boy because his parents, Mary and Joseph, had always taken him and thought it was important to go. Jesus even spent time there when he didn't have to.

Tell this story, with the children repeating '*They were on a journey*' every time you say it or variations of it.

‘When Jesus was a child, perhaps a bit older than most of you, a large number of people would often go to the temple in Jerusalem and worship there. Some travelled for days to gather there. It was like a really big meeting of most of the people who wanted to worship God from throughout the area. Jesus set off with his family, determined to get there in time – they were on a journey. As they walked for a day along the dusty and stony track more and more people joined them. No one particularly noticed Jesus – he was just like any other boy in the large crowd.

As they got nearer Jerusalem they could see that thousands of others were on a journey too, and the city was getting very busy indeed. They were all on a journey to the temple to celebrate God’s love for them and to enjoy being together.

The weekend soon passed, and it was time for everyone to go on the journey back home. Mary and Joseph, Jesus’ parents, got their things together and said many sad farewells to friends they had met and made. Then they joined the large crowd again, on a journey along the roads and tracks back home. It was a while later, perhaps a few hours, when Mary said to Joseph: ‘Where’s Jesus?’ They looked at each other, and then at the crowd. No one remembered seeing him that morning, and they had no idea where he was. In a flash Mary and Joseph were on a journey back to Jerusalem, determined to find their precious son.

They got back to the city late in the afternoon and walked up and down the main streets and squares, shouting his name and looking everywhere. In desperation they decided to look in at the temple, just in case any of the priests had seen him. There Jesus was, sitting talking to the priests and amazing them with all he knew about Father God and the Bible. 'This is where I like to be,' he said to his parents. 'This is where I belong.' All together Joseph, Mary and Jesus set off on the journey back home. ❜

Conclusion Bring out the fact that Jesus enjoyed being in the place where he could learn more about God and worship him. It is good for us to learn more, and to spend time with others. We do that in clubs, groups and in school, where we all belong. (*Hold up membership card*) I belong to _______ , and we all belong somewhere.

Prayer Ask the children to think of the clubs and places they belong to.
Then say this prayer:
Thank you, Jesus, for all of us here.
Thank you that we can learn and enjoy ourselves together.
Thank you for all the groups and clubs we belong to.
Thank you that you want us to be together.
Amen.

Object: Photo
Theme: Friends

10

Theme Friends are important and we should look after ours!

You will need A photo of a friend, old newspaper or mats.

Game *Blindfold identity*

Blindfold two or three children at the front. Pick out some of their friends from the group, not telling them who they are. The blindfolded children must identify the others by touching them. Allow only a short time for each identification.

Introduction This is a photo of my friend _______ . I met him/her _______ (*Here you may want to add one or two reasons why you are friends, and what you do together*) How many of you have got friends? How many of you have changed your friends in the last few days? Real friendships don't change every few days, and some friendships last a whole lifetime.

Active game *You can't be my friend*

Have a group of up to 15 children at the front. Put out sheets of newspaper or small mats on the floor. Play some music, asking the children to move around the room while the music plays. When the music stops they must all stand with both feet completely on the paper. Any who are not able to do this are '*not your friend*' and must sit out for the remaining time of the game.

As the children drop out and the music is played again remove a sheet of paper each time.

Discussion Ask the children to think back to the game and talk about how easy it was to identify the people. Some would have been easier than others, and some obvious to some children but not to others. Ask how many children think they know all of the names of those in their:

Class

Year at school

Club/activity outside school

We all need friends, and many of us have a lot of friends. But not everyone can be our friends, and we can't be friends with everyone. But we all need friends – even the headteacher, and even Jesus!

Story *Jesus invites people to be his friends*

Read out this account of what happened, explaining that it is from Simon Peter's point of view. He became one of Jesus' disciples, or special friends.

> ‘It was just another working day for me and the lads. We were heading in to the shore to sort the boat out and mend a few nets when we saw that man Jesus there with a small crowd.
>
> I'd never really listened to what he was saying, but loads of people thought he was some sort of messenger from God, or even God himself! I wasn't interested as we'd had a bad night with no fish, and I was tired.
>
> When Jesus came up and asked me to take him

out a little way in one of my boats I almost told him to forget it, but something about him made me say yes. From a short distance Jesus continued talking to the people and telling them lots of clever things which I didn't really understand. Once he'd finished I thought 'Good, now I can get home', but instead he told me to go further out to where the water was deeper and catch some fish.

By now I was not happy. I am the fisherman, not him! But I thought it was worth a try, and we threw the nets in. Well, they were so full of fish that when we pulled them in, the boat almost went over!

In a flash I knew Jesus was special and I was not good enough to be near him, let alone his friend. But Jesus said 'Come with me as my friend, and we'll do lots of good things for others.'

I knew I wanted to, and from that day on Jesus was my friend and he changed me completely! ’

Talk We all need friends, and it's exciting to have friends. But like anything that is special, we should look after our friends and do our best for them. If we do, they may be our best friends for a very long time.

Prayer Invite the children to spend some time thinking about the story of Simon Peter and how Jesus wanted Simon Peter to be his friend.

Ask the children to listen carefully to this prayer, thinking about Jesus' friendship for Simon Peter and their friends. If they agree with it to say 'Amen' at the end:

Thank you, Jesus, that you know everyone and you love us all.

Thank you, Jesus, that you know me and love me.

Thank you, Jesus, that you have given me friends.

Help me to be a good friend.

Amen.

Object: Tape recorder
Theme: **Power** 11

Theme We all need power to help us.

You will need A tape / CD player and socket point.

Introduction (*Have the tape/CD player unplugged*) I thought I would play some music now that you are all in and sitting ready to begin. So here we go, I'll press 'play'. Oh, nothing's happening, I wonder why? It needs to be plugged in properly! (*Check that the lead is in the back of the tape recorder*) Right, now it should work. Oh dear, I'll try plugging it in to my mouth . . . ear . . . the chair . . . etc. What does it need to make it work? Power! That's right. So if I plug it into the power point like this it should work at last. Yes, here we are! (*Play loud music for a short while*)

Quiz game *What power does*

Ask the children to think for a moment about what power is and what it does. Remind them that all engines and motors need power to make them go, whether it comes from petrol, steam, electricity, or anything else! Then try to come up with one thing power does or something power makes work beginning with each letter of the alphabet. Suggestions may include:

Ambulance

Battery

Car

Discussion

Talk through each of these points in turn, asking the children for suggestions of other people or things that are appropriate for each one.

Powerful
The headteacher at school has power, and so do our politicians and leaders. God is very powerful. Some people believe that he made the world, everything in it, and us too! They believe that he is in control of the weather, the mountains and seas, and that he is in control of everything!

Greatness
Some people are really great people. They may be sportsmen and women who have worked really hard and done really well, or people who do many good things for others.

Timeless
Some great people from the past are always going to be remembered. People will remember Julius Caesar, Florence Nightingale or Jesus. God described himself as being beyond time. He was here before time started and will be here after time itself ends.

Loving
Some people are really loving, and care for everyone around them. They might be like the loving people who look after you. God is described as being a loving Father.

Story

These are the main points of the story, to be elaborated depending on time. It may be appropriate to get a child out to improvise the actions of Moses. Use the response '*Moan, moan, moan*' every time the people moan in the narrative.

> ‘The people of Israel were special to God, and he didn't want them to be slaves in Egypt. They hated being slaves, and moaned about it.

After lots of things happened, far too many to mention in this story, God spoke to Moses. Moses was to be a great leader as long as he did what God said. At last, with Moses in charge, the people got away from being slaves.

They had escaped, but then the King of Egypt had changed his mind and sent his army to catch them. The people of Israel reached the Red Sea and couldn't escape. There were no boats, bridges or tunnels! They moaned, fearing that the army would catch them and kill them.

Moses prayed, held out his arm, and God held back the water for them all to cross in safety. The army behind them were destroyed.

On the other side they were thirsty, but the only water they found tasted foul. They moaned about the taste of the water.

Moses prayed and God changed the water so they could drink it, and provided springs of fresh water for them the next day.

The people became hungry. They moaned that they might starve to death. God sent down some manna, which was like bread. It landed on the ground along with small birds called quails. The people then had plenty to eat.

Moses had the power to be a great leader, and God had the power to help the people, even though they still moaned! ❜

This story is from the Bible, and demonstrates the power of God. He used his power to care for people. His power didn't come from engines or fuel – he has it always. But we all have power. We can all try harder and do things better if we really want to!

Prayer idea

Ask the children to think about all the things that power makes happen, including the tape recorder. Then ask them to think about things about themselves that they would like to change. Remind them that we all have the power to change.

Object: Men's shoes
Theme: Fathers
12

Theme

Fathers matter, even if they make mistakes.

You will need

A pair of men's shoes.

Active game

The king

Ask for five volunteers. Each one should act out one of these moody kings, while all the other children try to guess what mood the king may be in. You may want to add other moods to this list and use more volunteers.

Sad king
Generous king
Angry king
Happy king
Frightened king

Introduction

These shoes could have been worn by any kind of father. They could have been worn by a father who is at home to look after his children, who is loving and caring, and who gets most things right. They could have been worn by a father who is bossy and thinks he is a king, and king of the family. They could have been worn by a father who lives somewhere else and sees his children sometimes. Or they could have been worn by a father who is not around any more, who may have died or gone away. Fathers come in all shapes and sizes, and they all make mistakes.

Game *Fathers*

Ask for two children to volunteer. Each one should say a word that describes a good father, then the other says another word, and so on. There should be no repetition and no hesitation for longer than a couple of seconds. It is wise to be aware and sensitive to the different situations in the group regarding fathers.

Story Read this introduction and story. You may want to ask a child to act it out as you tell it.

King David lived thousands of years ago in the area of the world we now call Israel. He had children of his own, but as well as that he became father to all the people. Most of the time he was a good and caring father to them all. This is King David's story.

> ‘David was the youngest in his family, and his older brothers didn't really take much notice of him. They used to tease him for being smaller than them, and give him all the nasty jobs to do around the farm. He wasn't very old when David had to go out night and day to look after some of the sheep on the hillsides overlooking their house. It was a boring job, but David did it well and cared for the sheep, finding the best grass for them to eat and looking for any sheep who were lost. Once he came upon a lion attacking the sheep. He quickly picked up a stone, put it in his sling, flung the stone at the lion and killed it.
>
> One of the other jobs David had was to see how his brothers were doing and take them food.

There was a big battle going on, and his brothers were standing with the others in the army, wondering how they could fight the giant on the other side, who was called Goliath. David decided that with God on his side he could kill the giant, so without any armour he faced Goliath, who laughed at him. David used his sling to deadly effect again, striking Goliath hard on his head with a sharp stone so that he collapsed and died.

Despite David winning the battle, and playing the harp for the king, King Saul still hated him and tried to kill him. David had many years of hiding and hard work before he became king. He fought many battles, won many wars, and escaped many attacks. But even at the end of all his hard work he still cared for people. One day King Saul's grandson, Mephibosheth, came to King David expecting to be put to death. Instead, King David was kind to him and offered him riches. David was a brave boy, a strong and fearless young man, and a good and caring king – father to all the nation. ’

Game

David says . . .

Play '*David says . . .*' in the same way as you would play 'Simon says . . .' with some selected volunteers at the front. Ask the other children to watch and tell you when any of the volunteers goes wrong.

Give instructions which the children should follow as long as they are prefaced with '*David says . . .* .' The children who get it wrong are out.

Conclusion

David was powerful, yet even he was not as strong, powerful or caring a father to the people as his Father God. God was stronger than David, and sets all of us the best example of what a father can be. (*Hold up the shoes*) Your father may have worn these shoes, and your and my father got it wrong sometimes. The Father God sets an example of what fathers can be like, but it's not easy. So if you are in contact with your father forgive him his mistakes, he's probably doing his best!

Talk and discussion

Ask the children to sit quietly and think about fathers, both those they know and those they don't. If they want to, ask them to say 'Amen' after you have read this prayer:

Father God, we thank you for all who look after us.
We thank you for our fathers.
We ask you to help them be better ones.
Amen.

Object: Bread
Theme: Who is Jesus? 13

Theme God the Son is Jesus, who came to earth and grew as a child.

You will need A loaf of bread, a sheet with '*Speaker*' written on it, and another with '*Doer*' on it.

Introduction What can we do with this loaf of bread? What would happen if we left it here and looked at it for a week or two? Would that do us any good? Bread is for eating, and as we eat it we are filled up and it does us good. Listen out for when bread is mentioned later.

Game *Jesus is . . .*

Ask for two or three children to come out and speak for ten seconds each, telling the others all they know about Jesus. If they do not manage to keep talking they are out and the next child has a go.

Active game *Speaker and doer*

Put two large sheets of paper on the wall at opposite ends of the room. Then talk to the children, asking them what they know about what Jesus did. The list of activities below shows that Jesus was a *Speaker* (speaking, teaching, telling) and a *Doer* (healing, walking, miracles). Remind the children of a number of miracles and sayings of Jesus, and then ask them to point to one side of the room or the other, depending on whether he was speaking or doing.

Healed a blind man	*(D)*
Told the rich man what to do	*(S)*
Spoke to a large crowd	*(S)*
Changed water into wine	*(D)*
Told a man's pain to go	*(S)*
Made fish and bread appear	*(D)*
Made the wind stop by speaking to it	*(S)*
Explained God's love	*(S)*
Touched a lame man	*(D)*
Called to Zacchaeus	*(S)*

Story

Blind Bartimaeus

Deliver this story in your own words, preferably with two children acting it out as you are telling it.

> ‘Jesus was, as usual, surrounded by a noisy and needy crowd as he walked into yet another village. There were people walking with crutches, with bandages, and in great need. All the time the noise was deafening, with everyone calling out the name of Jesus and begging him to help them and make them better. At the back of the crowd was a blind man who kept asking what was going on, but nobody was interested. Blind old Bartimaeus was always there, and people ignored him, spat at him and even trod on him as they hurried past.
>
> Bartimaeus shouted out to Jesus, hoping that

somehow his shouts would be heard. The others in the crowd wanted him to be quiet, and they told him to shut up and go away. They didn't want Jesus to be disturbed by a dirty old beggar. But Bartimaeus didn't stop, and despite the noise Jesus heard him and went to help.

Jesus spoke to the old beggar. Bart was sure that Jesus could make him see again, and he really trusted Jesus to do it. Jesus was filled with pity for the old man, and because Bartimaeus had real faith in Jesus his sight suddenly returned. Bartimaeus was amazed, but the crowd were puzzled. They didn't understand why Jesus should care about an old blind beggar. They didn't realise that Jesus cared about everyone. ’

Talk Recap the story, pointing out that Jesus really cared for Bartimaeus and paid attention to him despite the crowd around them both. Christians believe that God sent his Son to help all people in the same way, so that he could show his love. The things Jesus did, like the healings, teachings and his painful death, were to show how much he loved people. Jesus treated Bartimaeus as an individual, and that's how he treats everyone.

Quiz Here are some sayings of Jesus, with some wrong ones in there too. After you read each one out ask the children to vote on whether it is true or made up.

1	I am the light of the world	(*True*)
2	I am the colours of the rainbow	(*False*)
3	I am with you always	(*True*)
4	I am the vine and you are the branches	(*True*)

5	I am the real thing	(*False*)
6	I am the house for you to live in	(*False*)
7	I am the bread of life	(*True*)
8	I am the gate	(*True*)

Conclusion

Jesus described himself in many ways. One of those was as the bread of life (*hold up the bread*). He was saying that he was the best person to feed on, to listen to and obey. Anyone who fed on what he said and did would have a good life.

Jesus was a good man, and did good things. He called himself the Son of God.

Prayer

Thank you, Jesus, that you helped many people.

Thank you, Jesus, that you said many good things.

Thank you, Jesus, that you know me and you love me.

Amen.

Object: Police hat
Theme: Getting help 14

Theme We all need help from others sometimes.

You will need A police helmet or hat.

Introduction (*Put the helmet on a child*). If this really were a policeman/woman here, what sorts of questions could we ask them? What situations would they be able to help us out of? How can we tell that he or she is someone we can trust to help us?

We all get into situations where we need the help of others. Sometimes we have to trust that the person who helps us is honest and is going to do the best for us.

Active game *Piggy back relay race*

Bring two teams of two pairs of children to the front. The first pair in each team have to race, one child on the back of the other, to the far end of the room and back without the rider falling off. Then the next pair race, the winning team being the one that gets both pairs to the end and back first in a relay.

Illustration Ask two children to come out to the front and take part in a short demonstration. Ask them to sit on the floor back-to-back and then link their arms. They should now stand up by pushing against each other without going on to their knees or using their hands. If the first pair is not successful then choose another pair to give it a try. Once you have finished, explain to the children how that illustration and the previous game relied on people working together. You can't have a piggy back if no one will carry you, and you can't stand up as a linked pair unless you both push at the same time.

Talk and discussion

Talk about any times that the children have got lost. Perhaps you can remember an incident to tell them about from your own childhood. Explore some of the feelings involved in being lost, including loneliness, sorrow, fear, panic, and so on.

Story one

Sarah was not feeling too happy. She had got up too late, and had been rushing ever since. She didn't understand the work they had been doing in class that morning, and she'd left her reading book at home. As she stood on the playground she thought it couldn't get any worse. But then it did!

The boys were playing football near her as usual. They were Lee and his mob – Big Lee who bullied everyone and even seemed to scare the teachers! Lee and his mates were always a bit careless about where they kicked the ball, and today was no exception. Before she knew what was happening the ball hit her very hard right in her face, knocking off and smashing her glasses. Sarah held her face with both hands as it stung and bled a little where her glasses frames had punctured the skin. She looked around for help, but saw nothing to encourage her. The dinner lady was looking the other way, and some of the boys had already started playing again after giggling at Sarah without her glasses on. But then Sarah noticed Big Lee heading towards her looking concerned. He picked up what was left of her glasses and helped her inside, apologising for her injury as he did so. Sarah was amazed. She never thought her help would come from him! ’

Story two

Split the children into three groups, giving each group one of the following phrases to learn, to be repeated by them after you have said them:

They must be drunk!

This is great!

‘ After Jesus had died, come alive again and gone to heaven he had left his friends, the disciples. They were feeling lost and fed up, and they had no one to help them like Jesus had. One day the disciples were all gathered in an upstairs room and were ready to pray and sing together. They still worshipped God but wanted help. They had no idea that the promised helper, the Holy Spirit, was going to come then. As they sat there thinking about how much they missed Jesus, the disciples heard a sound like a rushing wind and saw what looked like flames settling on their heads. 'This is great!' they said to each other.

As soon as their help – the Holy Spirit – came, they began to speak in languages which they did not actually know! 'This is great!' they said again. There was a large crowd of people from different countries gathered in the streets and squares of the city for a celebration, and they were amazed to hear these local men speaking their own home languages. 'They must be drunk!' said some of them, but the disciples repeated 'This is great!' The disciples were amazed, and were enjoying the Holy Spirit. Some in the crowd insisted that the disciples must be drunk. 'They must be drunk!' they kept shouting, because it was too unbelievable to be really happening. But the disciples didn't worry, they knew this was the help from God. The Holy Spirit stayed with them and helped them from then on, and again they said 'This is great!' ’

Quiz Here are some questions to ask with the children split into the same two groups as earlier:

What was the help from God called?
(*Holy Spirit*)

Why was Sarah having a bad day?
(*Late, didn't understand work, forgot book*)

Why had the disciples got together?
(*Pray/talk*)

Who led the group of boys playing football?
(*Big Lee*)

What new ability had the disciples got?
(*Speak in languages*)

What happened to Sarah on the playground?
(*Ball hit her, broke glasses*)

What did some people think the disciples had been doing?
(*Drinking*)

Who did Sarah least expect to help her?
(*Big Lee*)

How long was the Holy Spirit with the disciples?

(*For ever*)

Conclusion

We all need help sometimes but there isn't usually a policeman or woman around to help us. The disciples trusted God to help them and he did by sending the Holy Spirit. But we've all got a part to play in helping others. There are many of us who could help each other in small ways by sharing, supporting or helping with difficult work. Sarah was surprised by the person who offered to help her. Could you surprise someone by offering help today? Think about it!

Object: Globe
Theme: The world

15

Theme The world is ours to look after.

You will need A globe or inflatable world.

Introduction *(Hold up the globe)* You have all seen this before, and we are on it now. Look at it very carefully and then close your eyes. Now imagine hundreds of other globes, with seas and land. Now think back to this globe, and imagine you are on a spaceship heading fast down towards the earth. Now you are able to pick out the shape of our country, and now this town/village, and now you see people . . . and yourself.

Open your eyes again. The world might seem remote or to do with something or someone else. But it's not, it's all about you and me!

Active game *Animals*

Get 12 children out to the front. Give each of them a piece of paper with the name of one of the six animals listed on it. Then give them 30 seconds to get into pairs of the same animal by making noises that the particular animal makes.

Cow	*Cat*
Dog	*Lion*
Sheep	*Chicken*

Game *Mirrors*

Ask all the children to sit in pairs facing each other, and number themselves 1 and 2 in each pair. Number 1 has to act out what they do from getting up to going to school each day, while number 2 has to copy it as if they were a mirror. Then 2 acts out all that they do from going home from school until bedtime, while 1 has to mirror every action.

Illustration Ask each child to look very carefully at the person they are sitting next to. No one will have seen someone the same as them. Some animals in species look the same, but all people are different. All people are individuals. Yet we are all part of the world we share.

Talk The world is special, there can be no doubt about that. Yet as people we are hurting it by taking away forests, by polluting streams and rivers, by destroying the air we all need to breathe by pumping gases and fumes into it.

None of us knows quite how the world came into being. There are theories about evolution, with people and animals all evolving from a tiny water creature and continuing to evolve. Some people say this wonderful, beautiful world was created by a bang occurring between a mixture of gases and rocks which were fused or stuck together, and that it has changed since. Different religions have theories and stories about how the world came into being too, and they also have things to say about the state of the world now.

Stories *Creation*

The Christian story of creation is well known. In the beginning there was nothing but God, who chose to make a world. Day by day for six days he added things – sea and sky, night and day, land and animals, trees and plants, and so on. Finally he created a man and a woman. That was the beginning, but things didn't stop there.

Adam and Eve

God made a wonderful world, which was perfect. On the last of the seven days of creation he sat back, looked at it and decided that it was really good. But God had also made a man and a woman, and it was not long before things started to go wrong. There was a tree which God had told them not to touch, but they did anyway. They ate the fruit and immediately realised that they had done wrong. Full of guilt, they tried to hide from God, but he knew that they had done wrong and had spoiled the perfect world he had made.

The Flood

Things went from bad to worse, and the children of Adam and Eve did evil things. God looked at the world he had made and saw only a few people who listened to him – a man called Noah and his family. He decided it was time to clean the world up, so he told Noah to build a big boat for himself, his family and two of every kind of animal. When the flood came the boat floated on the water for many days, and the world was clean again. But things still went wrong.

The Messiah

The people of God still failed to do what God wanted them to. They would often ignore him and tell lies. In the end God promised them a saviour – the Messiah – who would come and help those who would listen to him. The Messiah was God's own Son, Jesus. A few people listened to Jesus but most turned against him, and he was killed by being nailed to a wooden cross. But Jesus was not finished, and two days later he came alive again.

Talk In the Christian story of our world God made the world and man perfect, yet it all went wrong. Jesus came to put things right again. Every person who lives in the world now can put things right by looking after it, by caring for where we live and the area around it, and by doing our bit to stop pollution. The world goes on, and we should want it to get better.

Prayer *Dear God,*

Thank you for this world.

Thank you for its beauty and preciousness.

Thank you for the light and the dark, the sea and the land.

Thank you for animals, fish and birds.

Thank you that we share it.

Help us to look after our world.

Amen.

Printed in the United Kingdom by
Lightning Source UK Ltd., Milton Keynes
140626UK00001B/6/P

9 781844 172962